MARGARET ATWOOD

was born in Ottawa in 1939. She spent much of her early life in the northern Ontario and Quebec bush country and started writing at the age of five. A graduate from the University of Toronto, where she won a Woodrow Wilson Fellowship, with a Masters degree from Radcliffe College, she has travelled extensively and held a variety of jobs.

Margaret Atwood is Canada's most eminent novelist, poet and critic. Her first volume of poetry, *The Circle Game* (1966), won the Governor-General's Award. Since then she has published fourteen volumes of poetry and a study of Canadian Literature, *Survival*. Her first novel *The Edible Woman* was published in 1969, followed by *Surfacing*, *Lady Oracle*, *Life Before Man*, *Bodily Harm*, and *The Handmaid's Tale*, winner of both the Arthur C. Clarke Award for Science Fiction and the Governor-General's Award. It was also shortlisted for the Booker Prize – and is now a major film, screenplay by Harold Pinter, starring Faye Dunaway and Robert Duvall. She has also published three collections of short stories, *Dancing Girls*, *Bluebeard's Egg* and *Wilderness Tips*. *Cat's Eye*, published in 1989, was also shortlisted for the Booker Prize. Virago publish all Margaret Atwood's works of fiction as well as *Poems: 1965–1975* and *Poems: 1976–1986*.

Margaret Atwood lives in Toronto with the writer Graeme Gibson and their daughter.

Margaret Atwood

Poems

1976–1986

Published by VIRAGO PRESS Limited 1992
20–23 Mandela Street, Camden Town, London NW1 0HQ

Copyright © by Margaret Atwood 1987

First published in America by Houghton Mifflin, 1987
This edition offset from Houghton Mifflin first edition

The right of Margaret Atwood to be identified as author of this
Work has been identified by her in accordance with the Copyright,
Designs and Patents Act 1988.

This book was published in a different form by Oxford University
Press (Canada) in 1986.

Thanks to Jonathan Cape Limited for kind permission to publish
poems from *True Stories*, (1982) and *Interlunar*, (1984).

*A CIP Catalogue record for this book is available from the
British Library*

Printed in Great Britain by Cox & Wyman Ltd, Reading, Berkshire

Contents

From NOTES TOWARDS A POEM
THAT CAN NEVER BE WRITTEN

From *Interlunar* (1984)

From SNAKE POEMS

From INTERLUNAR

New Poems (1985–1986)

From

Two-Headed Poems

1978

A PAPER BAG

I make my head, as I used to,
out of a paper bag,
pull it down to the collarbone,

draw eyes around my eyes,
with purple and green
spikes to show surprise,
a thumb-shaped nose,

a mouth around my mouth
penciled by touch, then colored in
flat red.

With this new head, the body now
stretched like a stocking and exhausted could
dance again; if I made a
tongue I could sing.

An old sheet and it's Halloween;
but why is it worse or more
frightening, this pinface
head of square hair and no chin?

Like an idiot, it has no past
and is always entering the future
through its slots of eyes, purblind
and groping with its thick smile,
a tentacle of perpetual joy.

Paper head, I prefer you
because of your emptiness;
from within you any
word could still be said.

With you I could have
more than one skin,
a blank interior, a repertoire
of untold stories,
a fresh beginning.

THE WOMAN WHO COULD NOT LIVE
WITH HER FAULTY HEART

I do not mean the symbol
of love, a candy shape
to decorate cakes with,
the heart that is supposed
to belong or break;

I mean this lump of muscle
that contracts like a flayed biceps,
purple-blue, with its skin of suet,
its skin of gristle, this isolate,
this caved hermit, unshelled
turtle, this one lungful of blood,
no happy plateful.

All hearts float in their own
deep oceans of no light,
wetblack and glimmering,
their four mouths gulping like fish.
Hearts are said to pound:
this is to be expected, the heart's
regular struggle against being drowned.

But most hearts say, I want, I want,
I want, I want. My heart
is more duplicitous,
though no twin as I once thought.
It says, I want, I don't want, I
want, and then a pause.
It forces me to listen,

and at night it is the infra-red
third eye that remains open
while the other two are sleeping
but refuses to say what it has seen.

It is a constant pestering
in my ears, a caught moth, limping drum,
a child's fist beating
itself against the bedsprings:
I want, I don't want.
How can one live with such a heart?

Long ago I gave up singing
to it, it will never be satisfied or lulled.
One night I will say to it:
Heart, be still,
and it will.

FIVE POEMS FOR DOLLS

i

Behind glass in Mexico
this clay doll draws
its lips back in a snarl;
despite its beautiful dusty shawl,
it wishes to be dangerous.

ii

See how the dolls resent us,
with their bulging foreheads
and minimal chins, their flat bodies
never allowed to bulb and swell,
their faces of little thugs.

This is not a smile,
this glossy mouth, two stunted teeth;
the dolls gaze at us
with the filmed eyes of killers.

iii

There have always been dolls
as long as there have been people.
In the trash heaps and abandoned temples
the dolls pile up;
the sea is filling with them.

What causes them?
Or are they gods, causeless,
something to talk to
when you have to talk,
something to throw against the wall?

A doll is a witness
who cannot die,
with a doll you are never alone.

On the long journey under the earth,
in the boat with two prows,
there were always dolls.

iv

Or did we make them
because we needed to love someone
and could not love each other?

It was love, after all,
that rubbed the skins from their gray cheeks,
crippled their fingers,
snarled their hair, brown or dull gold.
Hate would merely have smashed them.

You change, but the doll
I made of you lives on,
a white body leaning
in a sunlit window, the features
wearing away with time,
frozen in the gaunt pose
of a single day,
holding in its plaster hand
your doll of me.

v

Or: all dolls come
from the land of the unborn,
the almost-born; each
doll is a future
dead at the roots,
a voice heard only
on breathless nights,
a desolate white memento.

Or: these are the lost children,
those who have died or thickened
to full growth and gone away.

The dolls are their souls or cast skins
which line the shelves of our bedrooms
and museums, disguised as outmoded toys,
images of our sorrow,
shedding around themselves
five inches of limbo.

FIVE POEMS FOR GRANDMOTHERS

i

In the house on the cliff
by the ocean, there is still a shell
bigger and lighter than your head, though now
you can hardly lift it.

It was once filled with whispers;
it was once a horn
you could blow like a shaman
conjuring the year,
and your children would come running.

You've forgotten you did that,
you've forgotten the names of the children
who in any case no longer run,
and the ocean has retreated,
leaving a difficult beach of gray stones
you are afraid to walk on.

The shell is now a cave
which opens for you alone.
It is still filled with whispers
which escape into the room,
even though you turn it mouth down.

This is your house, this is the picture
of your misty husband, these are your children, webbed
and doubled. This is the shell,
which is hard, which is still there,
solid under the hand, which mourns, which offers
itself, a narrow journey
along its hallways of cold pearl
down the cliff into the sea.

ii

It is not the things themselves
that are lost, but their use and handling.

The ladder first; the beach;
the storm windows, the carpets;

The dishes, washed daily
for so many years the pattern
has faded; the floor, the stairs, your own
arms and feet whose work
you thought defined you;

The hairbrush, the oil stove
with its many failures,
the apple tree and the barrels
in the cellar for the apples,
the flesh of apples; the judging
of the flesh, the recipes
in tiny brownish writing
with the names of those who passed them
from hand to hand: Gladys,
Lorna, Winnie, Jean.

If you could only have them back
or remember who they were.

iii

How little I know
about you finally:

The time you stood
in the nineteenth century
on Yonge Street, a thousand
miles from home, with a brown purse
and a man stole it.

Six children, five who lived.
She never said anything
about those births and the one death;
her mouth closed on a pain
that could neither be told nor ignored.

She used to have such a sense of fun.
Now girls, she would say
when we would tease her.
Her anger though, why
that would curl your hair,
though she never swore.
The worst thing she could say was:
Don't be foolish.

At eighty she had two teeth pulled out
and walked the four miles home
in the noon sun, placing her feet
in her own hunched shadow.

The bibbed print aprons, the shock
of the red lace dress, the pin
I found at six in your second drawer,
made of white beads, the shape of a star.
What did we ever talk about
but food, health and the weather?

Sons branch out, but
one woman leads to another.
Finally I know you
through your daughters,
my mother, her sisters,
and through myself:

Is this you, this edgy joke
I make, are these your long fingers,
your hair of an untidy bird,
is this your outraged
eye, this grip
that will not give up?

iv

Some kind of ritual
for your dwindling,
some kind of dragon, small,
benign and wooden
with two mouths to catch your soul
because it is wandering
like a lost child, lift it back safely.

But we have nothing; we say,
How is she?
Not so good, we answer,
though some days she's fine.

On other days you walk through
the door of the room in the house
where you've lived for seventy years
and find yourself in a hallway
you know you have never seen before.

Midnight, they found her
opening and closing the door
of the refrigerator:
vistas of day-old vegetables, the used bone
of an animal, and beyond that
the white ice road that leads north.

They said, Mother,
what are you doing here?

Nothing is finished
or put away, she said.
I don't know where I am.

Against the disappearance
of outlines, against
the disappearance of sounds,
against the blurring of the ears
and eyes, against the small fears
of the very old, the fear
of mumbling, the fear of dying,
the fear of falling downstairs,
I make this charm
from nothing but paper; which is good
for exactly nothing.

v

Goodbye, mother
of my mother, old bone
tunnel through which I came.

You are sinking down into
your own veins, fingers
folding back into the hand,

day by day a slow retreat
behind the disk of your face
which is hard and netted like an ancient plate.

You will flicker in these words
and in the words of others
for a while and then go out.

Even if I send them,
you will never get these letters.
Even if I see you again,

I will never see you again.

MARRYING THE HANGMAN

She has been condemned to death by hanging. A man may escape this death by becoming the hangman, a woman by marrying the hangman. But at the present time there is no hangman; thus there is no escape. There is only a death, indefinitely postponed. This is not fantasy, it is history.

*

To live in prison is to live without mirrors. To live without mirrors is to live without the self. She is living selflessly, she finds a hole in the stone wall and on the other side of the wall, a voice. The voice comes through darkness and has no face. This voice becomes her mirror.

*

In order to avoid her death, her particular death, with wrung neck and swollen tongue, she must marry the hangman. But there is no hangman, first she must create him, she must persuade this man at the end of the voice, this voice she has never seen and which has never seen her, this darkness, she must persuade him to renounce his face, exchange it for the impersonal mask of death, of official death which has eyes but no mouth, this mask of a dark leper. She must transform his hands so they will be willing to twist the rope around throats that have been singled out as hers was, throats other than hers. She must marry the hangman or no one, but that is not so bad. Who else is there to marry?

*

You wonder about her crime. She was condemned to death for stealing clothes from her employer, from the wife of her employer. She wished to make herself more beautiful. This desire in servants was not legal.

*

She uses her voice like a hand, her voice reaches through the wall, stroking and touching. What could she possibly have said that would have convinced him? He was not condemned to death, freedom awaited him. What was the temptation, the one that worked? Perhaps he wanted to live with a woman whose life he had saved, who had seen down into the earth but had nevertheless followed him back up to life. It was his only chance to be a hero, to one person at least, for if he became the hangman the others would despise him. He was in prison for wounding another man, on one finger of the right hand, with a sword. This too is history.

*

My friends, who are both women, tell me their stories, which cannot be believed and which are true. They are horror stories and they have not happened to me, they have not yet happened to me, they have happened to me but we are detached, we watch our unbelief with horror. Such things cannot happen to us, it is afternoon and these things do not happen in the afternoon. The trouble was, she said, I didn't have time to put my glasses on and without them I'm blind as a bat, I couldn't even see who it was. These things happen and we sit at a table and tell stories about them so we can finally believe. This is not fantasy, it is history, there is more than one hangman and because of this some of them are unemployed.

*

He said: the end of walls, the end of ropes, the opening of doors, a field, the wind, a house, the sun, a table, an apple.

She said: nipple, arms, lips, wine, belly, hair, bread, thighs, eyes, eyes.

They both kept their promises.

*

The hangman is not such a bad fellow. Afterwards he goes to the refrigerator and cleans up the leftovers, though he does not wipe up what he accidentally spills. He wants only the simple things: a chair, someone to pull off his shoes, someone to watch him while he talks, with admiration and fear, gratitude if possible, someone in whom to plunge himself for rest and renewal. These things can best be had by marrying a woman who has been condemned to death by other men for wishing to be beautiful. There is a wide choice.

*

Everyone said he was a fool.
Everyone said she was a clever woman.
They used the word *ensnare*.

*

What did they say the first time they were alone together in the same room? What did he say when she had removed her veil and he could see that she was not a voice but a body and therefore finite? What did she say when she discovered that she had left one locked room for another? They talked of love, naturally, though that did not keep them busy forever.

*

The fact is there are no stories I can tell my friends that will make them feel better. History cannot be erased, although we can soothe ourselves by speculating about it. At that time there were no female hangmen. Perhaps there have never been any, and thus no man could save his life by marriage. Though a woman could, according to the law.

*

He said: foot, boot, order, city, fist, roads, time, knife.

She said: water, night, willow, rope hair, earth belly, cave, meat, shroud, open, blood.

They both kept their promises.

NOTE: In eighteenth-century Québec the only way for someone under sentence of death to escape hanging was, for a man, to become a hangman, or, for a woman, to marry one. Françoise Laurent, sentenced to hang for stealing, persuaded Jean Coro-lère, in the next cell, to apply for the vacant post of executioner, and also to marry her.

FOUR SMALL ELEGIES

(1838, 1977)

i

BEAUHARNOIS

The bronze clock brought
with such care over the sea,
which ticked like the fat slow heart
of a cedar, of a grandmother,
melted and its hundred years
of time ran over the ice and froze there.

We are fixed by this frozen clock
at the edge of the winter forest.
Ten below zero.
Shouts in a foreign language
come down blue snow.

The women in their thin nightgowns
disappear wordlessly among the trees.
Here and there a shape,
a limp cloth bundle, a child
who could not keep up
lies sprawled face down in a drift
near the trampled clearing.

No one could give them clothes or shelter,
these were the orders.

We didn't hurt them, the man said,
we didn't touch them.

ii

BEAUHARNOIS, GLENGARRY

Those whose houses were burned
burned houses. What else ever happens
once you start?

        While the roofs plunged
into the root-filled cellars,
they chased ducks, chickens, anything
they could catch, clubbed their heads
on rock, spitted them, singed off the feathers
in fires of blazing fences,
ate them in handfuls, charred
and bloody.

        Sitting in the snow
in those mended plaids, rubbing their numb feet,
eating soot, still hungry,
they watched the houses die like
sunsets, like their own
houses. Again

those who gave the orders
were already somewhere else,
of course on horseback.

BEAUHARNOIS

Is the man here, they said,
where is he?

She didn't know, though
she called to him as they dragged her
out of the stone house by both arms
and fired the bedding.

He was gone somewhere with the other men,
he was not hanged, he came back later,
they lived in a borrowed shack.

A language is not words only,
it is the stories
that are told in it,
the stories that are never told.

He pumped himself for years
after that into her body
which had no feet
since that night, which had no fingers.
His hatred of the words
that had been done became children.

They did the best they could:
she fed them, he told them
one story only.

DUFFERIN, SIMCOE, GREY

This year we are making
nothing but elegies.
Do what you are good at,
our parents always told us,
make what you know.

This is what we are making,
these songs for the dying.
You have to celebrate something.
The nets rot, the boats rot, the farms
revert to thistle, foreigners
and summer people admire the weeds
and the piles of stones dredged from the fields
by men whose teeth were gone by thirty.

But the elegies are new and yellow,
they are not even made, they grow,
they come out everywhere,
in swamps, at the edges of puddles,
all over the acres
of parked cars, they are mournful
but sweet, like flowered hats
in attics we never knew we had.

We gather them, keep them in vases,
water them while our houses wither.

NOTE: After the failure of the uprising in Lower Canada (now Québec) in 1838, the British army and an assortment of volunteers carried out reprisals against the civilian population around Beauharnois, burning houses and barns and turning the inhabitants out into the snow. No one was allowed to give them shelter and many froze to death. The men were arrested as rebels; those who were not home were presumed to be rebels and their houses were burned.

The volunteers from Glengarry were Scots, most of them in Canada because their houses had also been burned during the Highland Clearances, an aftermath of the British victory at Culloden. Dufferin, Simcoe, and Grey are the names of three counties in Ontario, settled around this period.

TWO-HEADED POEMS

"Joined Head to Head, and still alive"
Advertisement for Siamese Twins,
Canadian National Exhibition, c. 1954

The heads speak sometimes singly, sometimes
together, sometimes alternately within a poem.
Like all Siamese twins, they dream of separation.

i

Well, we felt
we were almost getting somewhere
though how that place would differ
from where we've always been, we
couldn't tell you

and then this happened,
this joke or major quake, a rift
in the earth, now everything
in the place is falling south
into the dark pit left by Cincinnati
after it crumbled.

This rubble is the future,
pieces of bureaucrats, used
bumper stickers, public names
returnable as bottles.
Our fragments made us.

What will happen to the children,
not to mention the words
we've been stockpiling for ten years now,
defining them, freezing them, storing
them in the cellar.
Anyone asked us who we were, we said
just look down there.

So much for the family business.
It was too small anyway
to be, as they say, viable.

But we weren't expecting this,
the death of shoes, fingers
dissolving from our hands,
atrophy of the tongue,
the empty mirror,
the sudden change
from ice to thin air.

ii

Those south of us are lavish
with their syllables. They scatter, we
hoard. Birds
eat their words, we eat
each other's, words, hearts, what's
the difference? In hock

up to our eyebrows, we're still
polite, god knows, to the tourists.
We make tea properly and hold the knife
the right way.

Sneering is good for you
when someone else has cornered
the tree market.

Who was it told us
so indelibly,
those who take risks
have accidents?

iii

We think of you as one
big happy family, sitting around
an old pine table, trading
in-jokes, hospitable to strangers
who come from far enough away.

As for us, we're the neighbors,
we're the folks whose taste
in fences and pink iron lawn flamingoes
you don't admire.

(All neighbors are barbarians,
that goes without saying,
though you too have a trashcan.)

We make too much noise,
you know nothing about us,
you would like us to move away.

Come to our backyard, we say,
friendly and envious,
but you don't come.

Instead you quarrel
among yourselves, discussing
genealogies and the mortgage,
while the smoke from our tireless barbecues
blackens the roses.

iv

The investigator is here,
proclaiming his own necessity.
He has come to clean your heart.

Is it pure white,
or is there blood in it?

Stop this heart!
Cut this word from his mouth.
Cut this mouth.

>   (Expurgation: purge.
>   To purge is to clean,
>   also to kill.)

For so much time, our history
was written in bones only.

Our flag has been silence,
which was mistaken for no flag,
which was mistaken for peace.

v

Is this what we wanted,
this politics, our hearts
flattened and strung out
from the backs of helicopters?

We thought we were talking
about a certain light
through the window of an empty room,
a light beyond the wet black trunks
of trees in this leafless forest
just before spring,
a certain loss.

We wanted to describe the snow,
the snow here, at the corner
of the house and orchard
in a language so precise
and secret it was not even
a code, it was snow,
there could be no translation.

To save this language
we needed echoes,
we needed to push back
the other words, the coarse ones
spreading themselves everywhere
like thighs or starlings.

No forests of discarded
crusts and torn underwear for us.
We needed guards.

Our hearts are flags now,
they wave at the end of each
machine we can stick them on.
Anyone can understand them.

They inspire pride,
they inspire slogans and tunes
you can dance to, they are redder than ever.

vi

Despite us
there is only one universe, the sun

burns itself slowly out no matter
what you say, is that
so?   The man
up to his neck in whitehot desert
sand disagrees.

Close your eyes now, see:
red sun, black sun, ordinary
sun, sunshine, sun-
king, sunlight soap, the sun
is an egg, a lemon, a pale eye,
a lion, sun
on the beach, ice on the sun.

Language, like the mouths
that hold and release
it, is wet & living, each

word is wrinkled
with age, swollen
with other words, with blood, smoothed by the numberless
flesh tongues that have passed across it.

Your language hangs around your neck,
a noose, a heavy necklace;
each word is empire,
each word is vampire and mother.

As for the sun, there are as many
suns as there are words for sun;

false or true?

vii

Our leader
is a man of water
with a tinfoil skin.

He has two voices,
therefore two heads, four eyes,
two sets of genitals, eight
arms and legs and forty
toes and fingers.
Our leader is a spider,

he traps words.
They shrivel in his mouth,
he leaves the skins.

Most leaders speak
for themselves, then
for the people.

Who does our leader speak for?
How can you use two languages
and mean what you say in both?

No wonder our leader skuttles
sideways, melts in hot weather,
corrodes in the sea, reflects
light like a mirror,
splits our faces, our wishes,
is bitter.

Our leader is a monster
sewn from dead soldiers,
a Siamese twin.

Why should we complain?
He is ours and us,
we made him.

viii

If I were a foreigner, as you say,
instead of your second head,
you would be more polite.

Foreigners are not there:
they pass and repass through the air
like angels, invisible
except for their cameras, and the rustle
of their strange fragrance

but we are not foreigners
to each other; we are the pressure
on the inside of the skull, the struggle
among the rocks for more room,
the shove and giveway, the grudging love,
the old hatreds.

Why fear the knife
that could sever us, unless
it would cut not skin but brain?

ix

You can't live here without breathing
someone else's air,
air that has been used to shape
these hidden words that are not yours.

This word was shut
in the mouth of a small man
choked off by the rope and gold/
red drumroll
This word was deported

This word was guttural,
buried wrapped in a leather throat
wrapped in a wolfskin

This word lies
at the bottom of a lake
with a coral bead and a kettle

This word was scrawny,
denied itself from year
to year, ate potatoes,
got drunk when possible

This word died of bad water.

Nothing stays under
forever, everyone
wants to fly, whose language
is this anyway?

You want the air
but not the words that come with it:
breathe at your peril.

These words are yours,
though you never said them,
you never heard them, history
breeds death but if you kill
it you kill yourself.

What is a traitor?

x

This is the secret: these hearts
we held out to you, these party
hearts (our hands
sticky with adjectives
and vague love, our smiles
expanding like balloons)

, these candy hearts we sent you
in the mail, a whole
bouquet of hearts, large as a country,

these hearts, like yours,
hold snipers.

A tiny sniper, one in each heart,
curled like a maggot, pallid
homunculus, pinhead, glass-eyed fanatic,
waiting to be given life.

Soon the snipers will bloom
in the summer trees, they will eat
their needle holes through your windows

(Smoke and broken leaves, up close
what a mess, wet red glass
in the zinnia border,
Don't let it come to this, we said
before it did.)

Meanwhile, we refuse
to believe the secrets of our hearts,
these hearts of neat velvet,
moral as fortune cookies.

Our hearts are virtuous, they swell
like stomachs at a wedding,
plump with goodwill.

In the evenings the news seeps in
from foreign countries,
those places with unsafe water.
We listen to the war, the wars,
any old war.

xi

Surely in your language
no one can sing, he said, one hand
in the small-change pocket.

That is a language for ordering
the slaughter and gutting of hogs, for
counting stacks of cans. Groceries
are all you are good for. Leave
the soul to us. Eat shit.

In these cages, barred crates,
feet nailed to the floor, soft
funnel down the throat,
we are forced with nouns, nouns,
till our tongues are sullen and rubbery.
We see this language always
and merely as a disease
of the mouth. Also
as the hospital that will cure us,
distasteful but necessary.

These words slow us, stumble
in us, numb us, who
can say even Open
the door, without these diffident
smiles, apologies?

Our dreams though
are of freedom, a hunger
for verbs, a song
which rises liquid and effortless,
our double, gliding beside us
over all these rivers, borders,
over ice or clouds.

Our other dream: to be mute.

Dreams are not bargains,
they settle nothing.

This is not a debate
but a duet
with two deaf singers.

THE BUS TO ALLISTON, ONTARIO

Snow packs the roadsides, sends dunes
onto the pavement, moves
through vision like a wave or sandstorm.
The bus charges this winter,
a whale or blunt gray
tank, wind whipping its flank.

Inside, we sit wool-
swathed and over-furred, made stodgy
by the heat, our boots
puddling the floor, our Christmas bundles
stuffed around us in the seats, the paper bags
already bursting; we trust

the driver, who is plump and garrulous, familiar
as a neighbor, which he is
to the thirty souls he carries, as
carefully as the time-
table permits; he knows
by experience the fragility of skulls.

Travel is dangerous; nevertheless, we travel.
The talk, as usual,
is of disasters; trainwrecks, fires,
herds of cattle killed in floods,
the malice of weather and tractors,
the clogging of hearts known
and unknown to us, illness and death,
true cases of buses

such as ours,
which skid, which hurtle
through snake fences and explode
with no survivors.
The woman talking says she heard
their voices at the crossroad
one night last fall, and not
a drop taken.

The dead ride with us on this bus,
whether we like it or not,
discussing aunts and suicides,
wars and the price of wheat,
fogging the close air, hugging us,
repeating their own deaths through these mouths,
cramped histories, violent
or sad, earthstained, defeated, proud,
the pain in small print, like almanacs,
mundane as knitting.

In the darkness, each distant house
glows and marks time,
is as true in attics
and cellars as in its steaming rich
crackling and butter kitchens.
The former owners, coupled and multiple,
seep through the mottled plaster, sigh
along the stairs they once rubbed concave
with their stiff boots, still envious,
breathe roasts and puddings through the floors;
it's wise
to set an extra plate.
How else can you live but with the knowledge
of old lives continuing in fading
sepia blood under your feet?

Outside, the moon is fossil
white, the sky cold purple, the stars
steely and hard; when there are trees they are dried
coral; the snow
is an unbroken spacelit
desert through which we make
our ordinary voyage,
those who hear voices and those
who do not, moving together, warm
and for the moment safe,
along the invisible road towards home.

THE WOMAN MAKES PEACE
WITH HER FAULTY HEART

It wasn't your crippled rhythm
I could not forgive, or your dark red
skinless head of a vulture

but the things you hid:
five words and my lost
gold ring, the fine blue cup
you said was broken,
that stack of faces, gray
and folded, you claimed
we'd both forgotten,
the other hearts you ate,
and all that discarded time you hid
from me, saying it never happened.

There was that, and the way
you would not be captured,
sly featherless bird, fat raptor
singing your raucous punctured song
with your talons and your greedy eye
lurking high in the molten sunset
sky behind my left cloth breast
to pounce on strangers.

How many times have I told you:
The civilized world is a zoo,
not a jungle, stay in your cage.
And then the shouts
of blood, the rage as you threw yourself
against my ribs.

As for me, I would have strangled you
gladly with both hands,
squeezed you closed, also
your yelps of joy.
Life goes more smoothly without a heart,
without that shiftless emblem,
that flyblown lion, magpie, cannibal
eagle, scorpion with its metallic tricks
of hate, that vulgar magic,
that organ the size and color
of a scalded rat,
that singed phoenix.

But you've shoved me this far,
old pump, and we're hooked
together like conspirators, which
we are, and just as distrustful.
We know that, barring accidents,
one of us will finally
betray the other; when that happens,
it's me for the urn, you for the jar.
Until then, it's an uneasy truce,
and honor between criminals.

SOLSTICE POEM

i

A tree hulks in the living-
room, prickly monster, our hostage
from the wilderness, prelude
to light in this dark space of the year
which turns again toward the sun
today, or at least we hope so.

Outside, a dead tree
swarming with blue and yellow
birds; inside, a living one
that shimmers with hollow silver
planets and wafer faces,
salt and flour, with pearl
teeth, tin angels, a knitted bear.

This is our altar.

ii

Beyond the white hill which maroons us,
out of sight of the white
eye of the pond, geography

is crumbling, the nation
splits like an iceberg, factions
shouting Good riddance from the floes
as they all melt south,

with politics the usual
rats' breakfast.

All politicians are amateurs:
wars bloom in their heads like flowers
on wallpaper, pins strut on their maps.
Power is wine with lunch
and the right pinstripes.

There are no amateur soldiers.
The soldiers grease their holsters,
strap on everything
they need to strap, gobble their dinners.
They travel quickly and light.

The fighting will be local,
they know, and lethal.
Their eyes flick from target
to target: window, belly, child.
The goal is not to get killed.

iii

As for the women, who did not
want to be involved, they are involved.

It's that blood on the snow
which turns out to be not
some bludgeoned or machine-gunned
animal's, but your own
that does it.

Each has a knitting needle
stuck in her abdomen, a red pincushion
heart complete with pins,
a numbed body
with one more entrance than the world finds safe,
and not much money.

Each fears her children sprout
from the killed children of others.
Each is right.

Each has a father.
Each has a mad mother
and a necklace of lightblue tears.
Each has a mirror
which when asked replies Not you.

iv

My daughter crackles paper, blows
on the tree to make it live, festoons
herself with silver.
So far she has no use
for gifts.

What can I give her,
what armor, invincible
sword or magic trick, when that year comes?

How can I teach her
some way of being human
that won't destroy her?

I would like to tell her, Love
is enough, I would like to say,
Find shelter in another skin.

I would like to say, Dance
and be happy. Instead I will say
in my crone's voice, Be
ruthless when you have to, tell
the truth when you can,
when you can see it.

Iron talismans, and ugly, but
more loyal than mirrors.

v

In this house (in a dying orchard,
behind it a tributary
of the wilderness, in front a road),
my daughter dances
unsteadily with a knitted bear.

Her father, onetime soldier,
touches my arm.
Worn language clots our throats,
making it difficult to say
what we mean, making it
difficult to see.

Instead we sing in the back room, raising
our pagan altar
of oranges and silver flowers:
our fools' picnic, our signal,
our flame, our nest, our fragile golden
protest against murder.

Outside, the cries of the birds
are rumors we hear clearly
but can't yet understand. Fresh ice
glints on the branches.
                              In this dark
space of the year, the earth
turns again toward the sun, or

we would like to hope so.

MARSH, HAWK

Diseased or unwanted
trees, cut into pieces, thrown
away here, damp and soft in the sun, rotting and half-
covered with sand, burst truck
tires, abandoned, bottles and cans hit
with rocks or bullets, a mass grave,
someone made it, spreads on the
land like a bruise and we stand on it, vantage
point, looking out over the marsh.

Expanse of green
reeds, patches of water, shapes
just out of reach of the eyes,
the wind moves, moves it and it
eludes us, it is full
daylight. From the places
we can't see, the guttural swamp voices
impenetrable, not human,
utter their one-note
syllables, boring and
significant as oracles and quickly over.

It will not answer, it will not
answer, though we hit
it with rocks, there is a splash, the wind
covers it over; but
intrusion is not what we want,

we want it to open, the marsh rushes
to bend aside, the water
to accept us, it is only
revelation, simple as the hawk
which lifts up now against
the sun and into
our eyes, wingspread and sharp call
filling the head/sky, this,

to immerse, to have it slide
through us, disappearance
of the skin, this is what we are looking for,
the way in.

A RED SHIRT

(For Ruth)

i

My sister and I are sewing
a red shirt for my daughter.
She pins, I hem, we pass the scissors
back & forth across the table.

Children should not wear red,
a man once told me.
Young girls should not wear red.

In some countries it is the color
of death; in others passion,
in others war, in others anger,
in others the sacrifice

of shed blood. A girl should be
a veil, a white shadow, bloodless
as a moon on water; not
dangerous; she should

keep silent and avoid
red shoes, red stockings, dancing.
Dancing in red shoes will kill you.

ii

But red is our color by birth-

right, the color of tense joy
& spilled pain that joins us

to each other. We stoop over
the table, the constant pull

of the earth's gravity furrowing
our bodies, tugging us down.

The shirt we make is stained
with our words, our stories.

The shadows the light casts
on the wall behind us multiply:

This is the procession
of old leathery mothers,

the moon's last quarter
before the blank night,

mothers like worn gloves
wrinkled to the shapes of their lives,

passing the work from hand to hand,
mother to daughter,

a long thread of red blood, not yet broken.

iii

Let me tell you the story
about the Old Woman.

First: she weaves your body.
Second: she weaves your soul.

Third: she is hated & feared,
though not by those who know her.

She is the witch you burned
by daylight and crept from your home

to consult & bribe at night. The love
that tortured you you blamed on her.

She can change her form,
and like your mother she is covered with fur.

The black Madonna
studded with miniature

arms & legs, like tin stars,
to whom they offer agony

and red candles when there is no other
help or comfort, is also her.

iv

It is January, it's raining, this gray
ordinary day. My
daughter, I would like
your shirt to be just a shirt,
no charms or fables. But fables
and charms swarm here
in this January world,
entrenching us like snow, and few
are friendly to you; though
they are strong,
potent as viruses
or virginal angels dancing
on the heads of pins,
potent as the hearts
of whores torn out
by the roots because they were thought
to be solid gold, or heavy
as the imaginary
jewels they used to split
the heads of Jews for.

It may not be true
that one myth cancels another.
Nevertheless, in a corner
of the hem, where it will not be seen,
where you will inherit
it, I make this tiny
stitch, my private magic.

v

The shirt is finished: red
with purple flowers and pearl
buttons. My daughter puts it on,

hugging the color
which means nothing to her
except that it is warm
and bright. In her bare

feet she runs across the floor,
escaping from us, her new game,
waving her red arms

in delight, and the air
explodes with banners.

NIGHT POEM

There is nothing to be afraid of,
it is only the wind
changing to the east, it is only
your father   the thunder
your mother   the rain

In this country of water
with its beige moon damp as a mushroom,
its drowned stumps and long birds
that swim, where the moss grows
on all sides of the trees
and your shadow is not your shadow
but your reflection,

your true parents disappear
when the curtain covers your door.
We are the others,
the ones from under the lake
who stand silently beside your bed
with our heads of darkness.
We have come to cover you
with red wool,
with our tears and distant whispers.

You rock in the rain's arms,
the chilly ark of your sleep,
while we wait, your night
father and mother,
with our cold hands and dead flashlight,
knowing we are only
the wavering shadows thrown
by one candle, in this echo
you will hear twenty years later.

ALL BREAD

All bread is made of wood,
cow dung, packed brown moss,
the bodies of dead animals, the teeth
and backbones, what is left
after the ravens. This dirt
flows through the stems into the grain,
into the arm, nine strokes
of the axe, skin from a tree,
good water which is the first
gift, four hours.

Live burial under a moist cloth,
a silver dish, the row
of white famine bellies
swollen and taut in the oven,
lungfuls of warm breath stopped
in the heat from an old sun.

Good bread has the salt taste
of your hands after nine
strokes of the axe, the salt
taste of your mouth, it smells
of its own small death, of the deaths
before and after.

Lift these ashes
into your mouth, your blood;
to know what you devour
is to consecrate it,
almost. All bread must be broken
so it can be shared. Together
we eat this earth.

YOU BEGIN

You begin this way:
this is your hand,
this is your eye,
that is a fish, blue and flat
on the paper, almost
the shape of an eye.
This is your mouth, this is an O
or a moon, whichever
you like. This is yellow.

Outside the window
is the rain, green
because it is summer, and beyond that
the trees and then the world,
which is round and has only
the colors of these nine crayons.

This is the world, which is fuller
and more difficult to learn than I have said.
You are right to smudge it that way
with the red and then
the orange: the world burns.

Once you have learned these words
you will learn that there are more
words than you can ever learn.
The word *hand* floats above your hand
like a small cloud over a lake.
The word *hand* anchors
your hand to this table,
your hand is a warm stone
I hold between two words.

This is your hand, these are my hands, this is the world,
which is round but not flat and has more colors
than we can see.

It begins, it has an end,
this is what you will
come back to, this is your hand.

54

From

True Stories

1981

TRUE STORIES

i

Don't ask for the true story;
why do you need it?

It's not what I set out with
or what I carry.

What I'm sailing with,
a knife, blue fire,

luck, a few good words
that still work, and the tide.

ii

The true story was lost
on the way down to the beach, it's something

I never had, that black tangle
of branches in a shifting light,

my blurred footprints
filling with salt

water, this handful
of tiny bones, this owl's kill;

a moon, crumpled papers, a coin,
the glint of an old picnic,

the hollows made by lovers
in sand a hundred

years ago: no clue.

iii

The true story lies
among the other stories,

a mess of colors, like jumbled clothing
thrown off or away,

like hearts on marble, like syllables, like
butchers' discards.

The true story is vicious
and multiple and untrue

after all. Why do you
need it? Don't ever

ask for the true story.

LANDCRAB I

A lie, that we come from water.
The truth is we were born
from stones, dragons, the sea's
teeth, as you testify,
with your crust and jagged scissors.

Hermit, hard socket
for a timid eye,
you're a soft gut scuttling
sideways, a blue skull,
round bone on the prowl.
Wolf of treeroots and gravelly holes,
a mouth on stilts,
the husk of a small demon.

Attack, voracious
eating, and flight:
it's a sound routine
for staying alive on edges.

Then there's the tide, and that dance
you do for the moon
on wet sand, claws raised
to fend off your mate,
your coupling a quick
dry clatter of rocks.
For mammals
with their lobes and tubers,
scruples and warm milk,
you've nothing but contempt.

Here you are, a frozen scowl
targeted in flashlight,
then gone: a piece of what
we are, not all,
my stunted child, my momentary
face in the mirror,
my tiny nightmare.

LANDCRAB II

The sea sucks at its own
edges, in and out with the moon.
Tattered brown fronds
(shredded nylon stockings,
feathers, the remnants of hands)
wash against my skin.

As for the crab, she's climbed
a tree and sticks herself
to the bark with her adroit
spikes; she jerks
her stalked eyes at me, seeing

a meat shadow,
food or a predator.
I smell the pulp
of her body, faint odor
of rotting salt,
as she smells mine,
working those martian palps:

seawater in leather.
I'm a category, a noun
in a language not human,
infra-red in moonlight,
a tidal wave in the air.

Old fingernail, old mother,
I'm up to scant harm
tonight; though you don't care,

you're no-one's metaphor,
you have your own paths
and rituals, frayed snails
and soaked nuts, waterlogged sacks
to pick over, soggy chips and crusts.

The beach is all yours, wordless
and ripe once I'm off it,
wading towards the moored boats
and blue lights of the dock.

POSTCARD

I'm thinking about you. What else can I say?
The palm trees on the reverse
are a delusion; so is the pink sand.
What we have are the usual
fractured Coke bottles and the smell
of backed-up drains, too sweet,
like a mango on the verge
of rot, which we have also.
The air clear sweat, mosquitoes
& their tracks; birds, blue & elusive.

Time comes in waves here, a sickness, one
day after the other rolling on;
I move up, it's called
awake, then down into the uneasy
nights but never
forward. The roosters crow
for hours before dawn, and a prodded
child howls & howls
on the pocked road to school.
In the hold with the baggage
there are two prisoners,
their heads shaved by bayonets, & ten crates
of queasy chicks. Each spring
there's a race of cripples, from the store
to the church. This is the sort of junk
I carry with me; and a clipping
about democracy from the local paper.

Outside the window
they're building the damn hotel,
nail by nail, someone's
crumbling dream. A universe that includes you
can't be all bad, but
does it? At this distance
you're a mirage, a glossy image
fixed in the posture
of the last time I saw you.
Turn you over, there's the place
for the address. Wish you were
here. Love comes
in waves like the ocean, a sickness which goes on
& on, a hollow cave
in the head, filling & pounding, a kicked ear.

NOTHING

Nothing like love to put blood
back in the language,
the difference between the beach and its
discrete rocks & shards, a hard
cuneiform, and the tender cursive
of waves; bone & liquid fishegg, desert
& saltmarsh, a green push
out of death. The vowels plump
again like lips or soaked fingers, and the fingers
themselves move around these
softening pebbles as around skin. The sky's
not vacant and over there but close
against your eyes, molten, so near
you can taste it. It tastes of
salt. What touches
you is what you touch.

From NOTES TOWARDS A POEM
THAT CAN NEVER BE WRITTEN

A CONVERSATION

The man walks on the southern beach
with sunglasses and a casual shirt
and two beautiful women.
He's a maker of machines
for pulling out toenails,
sending electric shocks
through brains or genitals.
He doesn't test or witness,
he only sells. My dear lady,
he says, You don't know
those people. There's nothing
else they understand. What could I do?
she said. Why was he at that party?

FLYING INSIDE YOUR OWN BODY

Your lungs fill & spread themselves,
wings of pink blood, and your bones
empty themselves and become hollow.
When you breathe in you'll lift like a balloon
and your heart is light too & huge,
beating with pure joy, pure helium.
The sun's white winds blow through you,
there's nothing above you,
you see the earth now as an oval jewel,
radiant & seablue with love.

It's only in dreams you can do this.
Waking, your heart is a shaken fist,
a fine dust clogs the air you breathe in;
the sun's a hot copper weight pressing straight
down on the thick pink rind of your skull.
It's always the moment just before gunshot.
You try & try to rise but you cannot.

TORTURE

What goes on in the pauses
of this conversation?
Which is about free will
and politics and the need for passion.

Just this: I think of the woman
they did not kill.
Instead they sewed her face
shut, closed her mouth
to a hole the size of a straw,
and put her back on the streets,
a mute symbol.

It doesn't matter where
this was done or why or whether
by one side or the other;
such things are done as soon
as there are sides

and I don't know if good men
living crisp lives exist
because of this woman or in spite
of her.
      But power
like this is not abstract, it's not concerned
with politics and free will, it's beyond slogans

and as for passion, this
is its intricate denial,
the knife that cuts lovers
out of your flesh like tumors,
leaving you breastless
and without a name,
flattened, bloodless, even your voice
cauterized by too much pain,

a flayed body untangled
string by string and hung
to the wall, an agonized banner
displayed for the same reason
flags are.

A WOMEN'S ISSUE

The woman in the spiked device
that locks around the waist and between
the legs, with holes in it like a tea strainer
is Exhibit A.

The woman in black with a net window
to see through and a four-inch
wooden peg jammed up
between her legs so she can't be raped
is Exhibit B.

Exhibit C is the young girl
dragged into the bush by the midwives
and made to sing while they scrape the flesh
from between her legs, then tie her thighs
till she scabs over and is called healed.
Now she can be married.
For each childbirth they'll cut her
open, then sew her up.
Men like tight women.
The ones that die are carefully buried.

The next exhibit lies flat on her back
while eighty men a night
move through her, ten an hour.
She looks at the ceiling, listens
to the door open and close.
A bell keeps ringing.
Nobody knows how she got here.

You'll notice that what they have in common
is between the legs. Is this
why wars are fought?
Enemy territory, no man's
land, to be entered furtively,
fenced, owned but never surely,
scene of these desperate forays
at midnight, captures
and sticky murders, doctors' rubber gloves
greasy with blood, flesh made inert, the surge
of your own uneasy power.

This is no museum.
Who invented the word *love*?

CHRISTMAS CAROLS

Children do not always mean
hope. To some they mean despair.
This woman with her hair cut off
so she could not hang herself
threw herself from a rooftop, thirty
times raped & pregnant by the enemy
who did this to her. This one had her pelvis
broken by hammers so the child
could be extracted. Then she was thrown away,
useless, a ripped sack. This one
punctured herself with kitchen skewers
and bled to death on a greasy
oilcloth table, rather than bear
again and past the limit. There
is a limit, though who knows
when it may come? Nineteenth-century
ditches are littered with small wax corpses
dropped there in terror. A plane
swoops too low over the fox farm
and the mother eats her young. This too
is Nature. Think twice then
before you worship turned furrows, or pay
lip service to some full belly
or other, or single out one girl to play
the magic mother, in blue
& white, up on that pedestal,
perfect & intact, distinct
from those who aren't. Which means
everyone else. It's a matter
of food & available blood. If mother-
hood is sacred, put
your money where your mouth is. Only
then can you expect the coming
down to the wrecked & shimmering earth
of that miracle you sing
about, the day
when every child is a holy birth.

NOTES TOWARDS A POEM
THAT CAN NEVER BE WRITTEN

(For Carolyn Forché)

i

This is the place
you would rather not know about,
this is the place that will inhabit you,
this is the place you cannot imagine,
this is the place that will finally defeat you

where the word *why* shrivels and empties
itself. This is famine.

ii

There is no poem you can write
about it, the sandpits
where so many were buried
& unearthed, the unendurable
pain still traced on their skins.

This did not happen last year
or forty years ago but last week.
This has been happening,
this happens.

We make wreaths of adjectives for them,
we count them like beads,
we turn them into statistics & litanies
and into poems like this one.

Nothing works.
They remain what they are.

iii

The woman lies on the wet cement floor
under the unending light,
needle marks on her arms put there
to kill the brain
and wonders why she is dying.

She is dying because she said.
She is dying for the sake of the word.
It is her body, silent
and fingerless, writing this poem.

iv

It resembles an operation
but it is not one

nor despite the spread legs, grunts
& blood, is it a birth.

Partly it's a job,
partly it's a display of skill
like a concerto.

It can be done badly
or well, they tell themselves.

Partly it's an art.

v

The facts of this world seen clearly
are seen through tears;
why tell me then
there is something wrong with my eyes?

To see clearly and without flinching,
without turning away,
this is agony, the eyes taped open
two inches from the sun.

What is it you see then?
Is it a bad dream, a hallucination?
Is it a vision?
What is it you hear?

The razor across the eyeball
is a detail from an old film.
It is also a truth.
Witness is what you must bear.

vi

In this country you can say what you like
because no one will listen to you anyway,
it's safe enough, in this country you can try to write
the poem that can never be written,
the poem that invents
nothing and excuses nothing,
because you invent and excuse yourself each day.

Elsewhere, this poem is not invention.
Elsewhere, this poem takes courage.
Elsewhere, this poem must be written
because the poets are already dead.

Elsewhere, this poem must be written
as if you are already dead,
as if nothing more can be done
or said to save you.

Elsewhere you must write this poem
because there is nothing more to do.

VULTURES

Hung there in the thermal
whiteout of noon, dark ash
in the chimney's updraft, turning
slowly like a thumb pressed down
on target; indolent V's; flies, until they drop.

Then they're hyenas, raucous
around the kill, flapping their black
umbrellas, the feathered red-eyed widows
whose pot bodies violate mourning,
the snigger at funerals,
the burp at the wake.

They cluster, like beetles
laying their eggs on carrion,
gluttonous for a space, a little
territory of murder: food
and children.

Frowzy old saint, bald-
headed and musty, scrawny-
necked recluse on your pillar
of blazing air which is not
heaven: what do you make
of death, which you do not
cause, which you eat daily?

I make life, which is a prayer.
I make clean bones.
I make a gray zinc noise
which to me is a song.

Well, heart, out of all this
carnage, could you do better?

SUNSET II

Sunset, now that we're finally in it
is not what we thought.

Did you expect this violet black
soft edge to outer space, fragile as blown ash
and shuddering like oil, or the reddish
orange that flows into
your lungs and through your fingers?
The waves smooth mouthpink light
over your eyes, fold after fold.
This is the sun you breathe in,
pale blue. Did you
expect it to be this warm?

One more goodbye,
sentimental as they all are.
The far west recedes from us
like a mauve postcard of itself
and dissolves into the sea.

Now there's a moon,
an irony. We walk
north towards no home,
joined at the hand.

I'll love you forever,
I can't stop time.

This is you on my skin somewhere
in the form of sand.

VARIATION ON THE WORD *SLEEP*

I would like to watch you sleeping,
which may not happen.
I would like to watch you,
sleeping. I would like to sleep
with you, to enter
your sleep as its smooth dark wave
slides over my head

and walk with you through that lucent
wavering forest of bluegreen leaves
with its watery sun & three moons
towards the cave where you must descend,
towards your worst fear

I would like to give you the silver
branch, the small white flower, the one
word that will protect you
from the grief at the center
of your dream, from the grief
at the center. I would like to follow
you up the long stairway
again & become
the boat that would row you back
carefully, a flame
in two cupped hands
to where your body lies
beside me, and you enter
it as easily as breathing in

I would like to be the air
that inhabits you for a moment
only. I would like to be that unnoticed
& that necessary.

MUSHROOMS

i

In this moist season,
mist on the lake and thunder
afternoons in the distance

they ooze up through the earth
during the night,
like bubbles, like tiny
bright red balloons
filling with water;
a sound below sound, the thumbs of rubber
gloves turned softly inside out.

In the mornings, there is the leaf mold
starred with nipples,
with cool white fishgills,
leathery purple brains,
fist-sized suns dulled to the color of embers,
poisonous moons, pale yellow.

ii

Where do they come from?

For each thunderstorm that travels
overhead there's another storm
that moves parallel in the ground.
Struck lightning is where they meet.

Underfoot there's a cloud of rootlets,
shed hairs or a bundle of loose threads
blown slowly through the midsoil.
These are their flowers, these fingers
reaching through darkness to the sky,
these eyeblinks
that burst and powder the air with spores.

iii

They feed in shade, on halfleaves
as they return to water,
on slowly melting logs,
deadwood. They glow
in the dark sometimes. They taste
of rotten meat or cloves
or cooking steak or bruised
lips or new snow.

iv

It isn't only
for food I hunt them
but for the hunt and because
they smell of death and the waxy
skins of the newborn,
flesh into earth into flesh.

Here is the handful
of shadow I have brought back to you:
this decay, this hope, this mouth-
ful of dirt, this poetry.

OUT

This is all you go with,
not much, a plastic bag
with a zipper, a bar of soap,
a command, blood in the sink,
the body's word.

You spiral out there,
locked & single
and on your way at last,
the rings of Saturn brilliant
as pain, your dark craft
nosing its way through stars.
You've been gone now
how many years?

Hot metal hurtles over your eyes,
razors the flesh, recedes;
this is the universe
too, this burnt view.

Deepfreeze in blankets; tubes feed you,
your hurt cells glow & tick;
when the time comes you will wake
naked and mended, on earth again, to find
the rest of us changed and older.

Meanwhile your body
hums you to sleep, you cruise
among the nebulae, ice glass
on the bedside table,
the shining pitcher, your white cloth feet
which blaze with reflected light
against the harsh black shadow
behind the door.

Hush, say the hands
of the nurses, drawing the blinds
down   hush
says your drifting blood,
cool stardust.

BLUE DWARFS

Tree burial, you tell me, that's
the way. Not up in but under.
Rootlets & insects, you say as we careen
along the highway with the news on
through a wind thickening with hayfever.
Last time it was fire.

It's a problem, what to do
with yourself after you're dead.
Then there's before.

The scabby wild plums fall from the tree
as I climb it, branches & leaves
peeling off under my bootsoles.
They vanish into the bone-colored
grass & mauve asters
or lie among the rocks and the stench
of woodchucks, bursting & puckered
and oozing juice & sweet pits & yellow
pulp but still
burning, cool and blue
as the cores of the old stars
that shrivel out there in multiples
of zero. Pinpoint mouths
burrowing in them. I pick up the good ones
which won't last long either.

If there's a tree for you it should be
this one. Here
it is, your six-quart basket
of blue light, sticky
and fading but more than
still edible. Time smears
our hands all right, we lick it off, a windfall.

LAST DAY

This is the last day of the last week.
It's June, the evenings touching
our skins like plush, milkweed sweetening
the sticky air which pulses
with moths, their powdery wings and velvet
tongues. In the dusk, nighthawks and the fluting
voices from the pond, its edges
webbed with spawn. Everything
leans into the pulpy moon.

In the mornings the hens
make egg after egg, warty-shelled
and perfect; the henhouse floor
packed with old shit and winter straw
trembles with flies, green and silver.

Who wants to leave it, who wants it
to end, water moving
against water, skin
against skin? We wade
through moist sun-
light towards nothing, which is oval

and full. This egg
in my hand is our last meal,
you break it open and the sky
turns orange again and the sun rises
again and this is the last day again.

From

Interlunar

1984

From SNAKE POEMS

SNAKE WOMAN

I was once the snake woman,

the only person, it seems, in the whole place
who wasn't terrified of them.

I used to hunt with two sticks
among milkweed and under porches and logs
for this vein of cool green metal
which would run through my fingers like mercury
or turn to a raw bracelet
gripping my wrist:

I could follow them by their odor,
a sick smell, acid and glandular,
part skunk, part inside
of a torn stomach,
the smell of their fear.

Once caught, I'd carry them,
limp and terrorized, into the dining room,
something even men were afraid of.
What fun I had!
Put that thing in my bed and I'll kill you.

Now, I don't know.
Now I'd consider the snake.

BAD MOUTH

There are no leaf-eating snakes.
All are fanged and gorge on blood.
Each one is a hunter's hunter,
nothing more than an endless gullet
pulling itself on over the still-alive prey
like a sock gone ravenous, like an evil glove,
like sheer greed, lithe and devious.

Puff adder buried in hot sand
or poisoning the toes of boots,
for whom killing is easy and careless
as war, as digestion,
why should you be spared?

And you, *Constrictor constrictor*,
sinuous ribbon of true darkness,
one long muscle with eyes and an anus,
looping like thick tar out of the trees
to squeeze the voice from anything edible,
reducing it to scales and belly.

And you, pit viper
with your venomous pallid throat
and teeth like syringes
and your nasty radar
homing in on the deep red shadow
nothing else knows it casts . . .
Shall I concede these deaths?

Between us there is no fellow feeling,
as witness: a snake cannot scream.
Observe the alien
chainmail skin, straight out
of science fiction, pure
shiver, pure Saturn.

Those who can explain them
can explain anything.

Some say they're a snarled puzzle
only gasoline and a match can untangle.
Even their mating is barely sexual,
a romance between two lengths
of cyanide-colored string.
Despite their live births and squirming nests
it's hard to believe in snakes loving.

Alone among the animals
the snake does not sing.
The reason for them is the same
as the reason for stars, and not human.

EATING SNAKE

I too have taken the god into my mouth,
chewed it up and tried not to choke on the bones.
Rattlesnake it was, panfried
and good too though a little oily.

(Forget the phallic symbolism:
two differences:
snake tastes like chicken,
and who ever credited the prick with wisdom?)

All peoples are driven
to the point of eating their gods
after a time: it's the old greed
for a plateful of outer space, that craving for darkness,
the lust to feel what it does to you
when your teeth meet in divinity, in the flesh,
when you swallow it down
and you can see with its own cold eyes,
look out through murder.

This is a lot of fuss to make about mere lunch:
metaphysics with onions.
The snake was not served with its tail in its mouth
as would have been appropriate.
Instead the cook nailed the skin to the wall,
complete with rattles, and the head was mounted.
It was only a snake after all.

(Nevertheless, the authorities are agreed:
God is round.)

METEMPSYCHOSIS

Somebody's grandmother glides through the bracken,
in widow's black and graceful
and sharp as ever: see how her eyes glitter!

Who were you when you were a snake?

This one was a dancer who is now
a green streamer waved by its own breeze
and here's your blunt striped uncle, come back
to bask under the wicker chairs
on the porch and watch over you.

Unfurling itself from its cast skin,
the snake proclaims resurrection
to all believers

though some tire soon of being born
over and over; for them there's the breath
that shivers in the yellow grass,
a papery finger, half of a noose, a summons
to the dead river.

Who's that in the cold cellar
with the apples and the rats? Whose is
that voice of a husk rasping in the wind?
Your lost child whispering *Mother*,
the one more child you never had,
your child who wants back in.

PSALM TO SNAKE

O snake, you are an argument
for poetry:

a shift among dry leaves
when there is no wind,
a thin line moving through

that which is not
time, creating time,
a voice from the dead, oblique

and silent. A movement
from left to right,
a vanishing. Prophet under a stone.

I know you're there
even when I can't see you

I see the trail you make
in the blank sand, in the morning

I see the point
of intersection, the whiplash
across the eye. I see the kill.

O long word, cold-blooded and perfect

QUATTROCENTO

The snake enters your dreams through paintings:
this one, of a formal garden
in which there are always three:

the thin man with the green-white skin
that marks him vegetarian
and the woman with a swayback and hard breasts
that look stuck on

and the snake, vertical and with a head
that's face-colored and haired like a woman's.

Everyone looks unhappy,
even the few zoo animals, stippled with sun,
even the angel who's like a slab
of flaming laundry, hovering
up there with his sword of fire,
unable as yet to strike.

There's no love here.
Maybe it's the boredom.

And that's no apple but a heart
torn out of someone
in this myth gone suddenly Aztec.

This is the possibility of death
the snake is offering:
death upon death squeezed together,
a blood snowball.

To devour it is to fall out
of the still unending noon
to a hard ground with a straight horizon

and you are no longer the
idea of a body but a body,
you slide down into your body as into hot mud.

You feel the membranes of disease
close over your head, and history
occurs to you and space enfolds
you in its armies, in its nights, and you
must learn to see in darkness.

Here you can praise the light,
having so little of it:

it's the death you carry in you
red and captured, that makes the world
shine for you
as it never did before.

This is how you learn prayer.

Love is choosing, the snake said.
The kingdom of God is within you
because you ate it.

AFTER HERACLITUS

The snake is one name of God,
my teacher said:
All nature is a fire
we burn in and are
renewed, one skin
shed and then another.

To talk with the body
is what the snake does, letter
after letter formed on the grass,
itself a tongue, looping its earthy hieroglyphs,
the sunlight praising it
as it shines there on the doorstep,
a green light blessing your house.

This is the voice
you could pray to for the answers
to your sickness:
leave it a bowl of milk,
watch it drink

You do not pray, but go for the shovel,
old blood on the blade

But pick it up and you would hold
the darkness that you fear
turned flesh and embers,
cool power coiling into your wrists
and it would be in your hands
where it always has been.

This is the nameless one
giving itself a name,
one among many

and your own name as well.

You know this and still kill it.

BEDSIDE

You sit beside the bed
in the *extremis* ward, holding your father's feet
as you have not done since you were a child.
You would hold his hands, but they are strapped down,
emptied at last of power.

He can see, possibly, the weave of the sheet
that covers him from chest to ankles;
he does not wish to.

He has been opened. He is at the mercy.

You hold his feet,
not moving. You would like
to drag him back. You remember
how you have judged each other
in silence, relentlessly.

You listen intently, as if for a signal,
to the undersea ping of the monitors,
the waterlogged lungs breathed into by machines,
the heart, wired for sound
and running too quickly in the stuck body,

the murderous body, the body
itself stalled in a field of ice
that spreads out endlessly under it,
the snowdrifts tucked by the wind around
the limbs and torso.

Now he is walking
somewhere you cannot follow,
leaving no footprints.
Already in this whiteness
he casts no shadow.

PRECOGNITION

Living backwards means only
I must suffer everything twice.
Those picnics were already loss:
with the dragonflies and the clear streams halfway.

What good did it do me to know
how far along you would come with me
and when you would return?
By yourself, to a life you call daily.

You did not consider me a soul
but a landscape, not even one
I recognize as mine, but foreign
and rich in curios:
an egg of blue marble,
a dried pod,
a clay goddess you picked up at a stall
somewhere among the dun and dust-green
hills and the bronze-hot
sun and the odd shadows,

not knowing what would be protection,
or even the need for it then.

I wake in the early dawn and there is the roadway
shattered, and the glass and blood,
from an intersection that has happened
already, though I can't say when.
Simply that it will happen.

What could I tell you now that would keep you
safe or warn you?
What good would it do?
Live and be happy.

I would rather cut myself loose
from time, shave off my hair
and stand at a crossroads
with a wooden bowl, throwing
myself on the dubious mercy
of the present, which is innocent
and forgetful and hits the eye bare

and without words and without even love
than do this mourning over.

KEEP

I know that you will die
before I do.

Already your skin tastes faintly
of the acid that is eating through you.

None of this, none of this is true,
no more than a leaf is botany,

along this avenue of old maples
the birds fall down through the branches
as the long slow rain of small bodies
falls like snow through the darkening sea,

wet things in turn move up out of the earth,
your body is liquid in my hands, almost
a piece of solid water.

Time is what we're doing,
I'm falling into the flesh,
into the sadness of the body
that cannot give up its habits,
habits of the hands and skin.

I will be one of those old women
with good bones and stringy necks
who will not let go of anything.

You'll be there. You'll keep
your distance,
the same one.

ANCHORAGE

This is the sea then, once
again, warm this time
and swarming. Sores fester
on your feet in the tepid
beach water, where French
wine bottles float among grape-
fruit peels and the stench of death
from the piles of sucked-out shells
and emptied lunches.
Here is a pool with nurse sharks
kept for the tourists
and sea turtles scummy with algae,
winging their way through their closed
heaven of dirty stones. Here
is where the good ship *Envious*
rides at anchor.
The land is red with hibiscus
and smells of piss; and here
beside the houses built on stilts,
warped in the salt and heat,
they plant their fathers in the yards,
cover them with cement
tender as blankets:

Drowned at sea, the same one
the mermaids swim in, hairy
and pallid, with rum on the beach after.
But that's a day trip.
Further along, there are tents
where the fishers camp,
cooking their stews of claws
and spines, and at dawn they steer
further out than you'd think
possible, between the killer
water and the killer sun,
carried on hollow pieces
of wood with the names of women,
not sweethearts
only but mothers, clumsy
and matronly, though their ribbed bodies
are fragile as real bodies
and like them also a memory,
and like them also two hands
held open, and like them also
the last hope of safety.

GEORGIA BEACH

In winter the beach is empty
but south, so there is no snow.

Empty can mean either
peaceful or desolate.

Two kinds of people walk here:
those who think they have love
and those who think they are without it.

I am neither one nor the other.

I pick up the vacant shells,
for which *open* means *killed*,
saving only the most perfect,
not knowing who they are for.

Near the water there are skinless
trees, fluid, grayed by weather,
in shapes of agony, or you could say
grace or passion as easily.
In any case twisted.

By the wind, which keeps going.
The empty space, which is not empty
space, moves through me.

I come back past the salt marsh,
dull yellow and rust-colored,
which whispers to itself,
which is sad only to us.

A SUNDAY DRIVE

The skin seethes in the heat
which roars out from the sun, wave after tidal wave;
the sea is flat and hot and too bright,
stagnant as a puddle,
edged by a beach reeking of shit.
The city is like a city
bombed out and burning;
the smell of smoke is everywhere,
drifting from the mounds of rubble.
Now and then a new tower,
already stained, lifts from the tangle;
the cars stall and bellow.
From the trampled earth rubbish erupts
and huts of tin and warped boards
and cloth and anything scavenged.
Everything is the color of dirt
except the kites, red and purple,
three of them, fluttering cheerfully
from a slope of garbage,
and the women's dresses, cleaned somehow,
vaporous and brilliant, and the dutiful
white smiles of the child beggars
who kiss your small change
and press it to their heads and hearts.

Uncle, they call you. *Mother.*
I have never felt less motherly.
The moon is responsible for all this,
goddess of increase
and death, which here are the same.
Why try to redeem
anything? In this maze
of condemned flesh without beginning or end
where the pulp of the body steams and bloats
and spawns and multiplies itself
the wise man chooses serenity.

Here you are taught the need to be holy,
to wash a lot and live apart.
Burial by fire is the last mercy:
decay is reserved for the living.

The desire to be loved is the last illusion:
Give it up and you will be free.

Bombay, 1982

ORPHEUS (1)

You walked in front of me,
pulling me back out
to the green light that had once
grown fangs and killed me.

I was obedient, but
numb, like an arm
gone to sleep; the return
to time was not my choice.

By then I was used to silence.
Though something stretched between us
like a whisper, like a rope:
my former name,
drawn tight.
You had your old leash
with you, love you might call it,
and your flesh voice.

Before your eyes you held steady
the image of what you wanted
me to become: living again.
It was this hope of yours that kept me following.

I was your hallucination, listening
and floral, and you were singing me:
already new skin was forming on me
within the luminous misty shroud
of my other body; already
there was dirt on my hands and I was thirsty.

I could see only the outline
of your head and shoulders,
black against the cave mouth,
and so could not see your face
at all, when you turned

and called to me because you had
already lost me. The last
I saw of you was a dark oval.
Though I knew how this failure
would hurt you, I had to
fold like a gray moth and let go.

You could not believe I was more than your echo.

EURYDICE

He is here, come down to look for you.
It is the song that calls you back,
a song of joy and suffering
equally: a promise:
that things will be different up there
than they were last time.

You would rather have gone on feeling nothing,
emptiness and silence; the stagnant peace
of the deepest sea, which is easier
than the noise and flesh of the surface.

You are used to these blanched dim corridors,
you are used to the king
who passes you without speaking.

The other one is different
and you almost remember him.
He says he is singing to you
because he loves you,

not as you are now,
so chilled and minimal: moving and still
both, like a white curtain blowing
in the draft from a half-opened window
beside a chair on which nobody sits.

He wants you to be what he calls real.
He wants you to stop light.
He wants to feel himself thickening
like a treetrunk or a haunch
and see blood on his eyelids
when he closes them, and the sun beating.

This love of his is not something
he can do if you aren't there,
but what you knew suddenly as you left your body
cooling and whitening on the lawn

was that you love him anywhere,
even in this land of no memory,
even in this domain of hunger.
You hold love in your hand, a red seed
you had forgotten you were holding.

He has come almost too far.
He cannot believe without seeing,
and it's dark here.
Go back, you whisper,

but he wants to be fed again
by you. O handful of gauze, little
bandage, handful of cold
air, it is not through him
you will get your freedom.

THE ROBBER BRIDEGROOM

He would like not to kill. He would like
what he imagines other men have,
instead of this red compulsion. Why do the women
fail him and die badly? He would like to kill them gently,
finger by finger and with great tenderness, so that
at the end they would melt into him
with gratitude for his skill and the final pleasure
he still believes he could bring them
if only they would accept him,
but they scream too much and make him angry.
Then he goes for the soul, rummaging
in their flesh for it, despotic with self-pity,
hunting among the nerves and the shards
of their faces for the one thing
he needs to live, and lost
back there in the poplar and spruce forest
in the watery moonlight, where his young bride,
pale but only a little frightened,
her hands glimmering with his own approaching
death, gropes her way towards him
along the obscure path, from white stone
to white stone, ignorant and singing,
dreaming of him as he is.

LETTER FROM PERSEPHONE

This is for the left-handed mothers
in their fringed black shawls or flowered housecoats
of the 'forties, their pink mule slippers,
their fingers, painted red or splay-knuckled
that played the piano formerly.

I know about your houseplants
that always died, about your spread
thighs roped down and split
between, and afterwards
that struggle of amputees
under a hospital sheet that passed
for sex and was never mentioned,
your invalid mothers, your boredom,
the enraged sheen of your floors;
I know about your fathers
who wanted sons.

These are the sons
you pronounced with your bodies,
the only words you could
be expected to say,
these flesh stutters.

No wonder this one
is nearly mute, flinches when touched,
is afraid of caves
and this one threw himself at a train
so he could feel his own heartbeat
once anyway; and this one
touched his own baby gently
he thought, and it came undone;
and this one enters the trussed bodies
of women as if spitting.

I know you cry at night
and they do, and they are looking for you.

They wash up here, I get
this piece or that. It's a blood
puzzle.

It's not your fault
either, but I can't fix it.

NO NAME

This is the nightmare you now have frequently:
that a man will come to your house at evening
with a hole in him — you place it
in the chest, on the left side — and blood leaking out
onto the wooden door as he leans against it.

He is a man in the act of vanishing
one way or another.
He wants you to let him in.
He is like the soul of a dead
lover, come back to the surface of the earth
because he did not have enough of it and is still hungry

but he is far from dead. Though the hair
lifts on your arms and cold
air flows over your threshold
from him, you have never
seen anyone so alive

as he touches, just touches your hand
with his left hand, the clean
one, and whispers *Please*
in any language.

You are not a doctor or anything like it.
You have led a plain life
which anyone looking would call blameless.
On the table behind you
there are bread on a plate, fruit in a bowl.
There is one knife. There is one chair.

It is spring, and the night wind
is moist with the smell of turned loam
and the early flowers;
the moon pours out its beauty
which you see as beauty finally,
warm and offering everything.
You have only to take.
In the distance you hear dogs barking.

Your door is either half open
or half closed.
It stays that way and you cannot wake.

ORPHEUS (2)

Whether he will go on singing
or not, knowing what he knows
of the horror of this world:

He was not wandering among meadows
all this time. He was down there
among the mouthless ones, among
those with no fingers, those
whose names are forbidden,
those washed up eaten into
among the gray stones
of the shore where nobody goes
through fear. Those with silence.

He has been trying to sing
love into existence again
and he has failed.

Yet he will continue
to sing, in the stadium
crowded with the already dead
who raise their eyeless faces
to listen to him; while the red flowers
grow up and splatter open
against the walls.

They have cut off both his hands
and soon they will tear
his head from his body in one burst
of furious refusal.
He foresees this. Yet he will go on
singing, and in praise.
To sing is either praise
or defiance. Praise is defiance.

THE WORDS CONTINUE
THEIR JOURNEY

Do poets really suffer more
than other people? Isn't it only
that they get their pictures taken
and are seen to do it?
The loony bins are full of those
who never wrote a poem.
Most suicides are not
poets: a good statistic.

Some days though I want, still,
to be like other people;
but then I go and talk with them,
these people who are supposed to be
other, and they are much like us,
except that they lack the sort of thing
we think of as a voice.
We tell ourselves they are fainter
than we are, less defined,
that they are what we are defining,
that we are doing them a favor,
which makes us feel better.
They are less elegant about pain than we are.

But look, I said *us*. Though I may hate your guts
individually, and want never to see you,
though I prefer to spend my time
with dentists because I learn more,
I spoke of us as *we*, I gathered us
like the members of some doomed caravan

which is how I see us, traveling together,
the women veiled and singly, with that inturned
sight and the eyes averted,
the men in groups, with their moustaches
and passwords and bravado

in the place we're stuck in, the place we've chosen,
a pilgrimage that took a wrong turn
somewhere far back and ended
here, in the full glare
of the sun, and the hard red-black shadows
cast by each stone, each dead tree lurid
in its particulars, its doubled gravity, but floating
too in the aureole of *stone*, of *tree*,

and we're no more doomed really than anyone, as we go
together, through this moon terrain
where everything is dry and perishing and so
vivid, into the dunes, vanishing out of sight,
vanishing out of the sight of each other,
vanishing even out of our own sight,
looking for water.

HEART TEST WITH AN ECHO CHAMBER

Wired up at the ankles and one wrist,
a wet probe rolling over my skin,
I see my heart on a screen
like a rubber bulb or a soft fig, but larger,

enclosing a tentative double flutter,
the rhythm of someone out of breath
but trying to speak anyway; two valves opening
and shutting like damp wings
unfurling from a gray pupa.

This is the heart as television,
a softcore addiction
of the afternoon. The heart
as entertainment, out of date
in black and white.
The technicians watch the screen,
looking for something: a block, a leak,
a melodrama, a future
sudden death, clenching
of this fist which goes on
shaking itself at fate.
They say: It may be genetic.

(There you have it, from science,
what God has been whispering all along
through stones, madmen and birds' entrails:
hardness of the heart can kill you.)
They change the picture:
now my heart is cross-sectioned
like a slice of textbook geology.
They freeze-frame it, take its measure.

A deep breath, they say.
The heart gasps and plods faster.
It enlarges, grows translucent,
a glowing stellar
cloud at the far end
of a starscope. A pear
made of smoke and about to rot.
For once the blood and muscle
heart and the heart of pure
light are beating in unison,
visibly.

Dressing, I am diaphanous,
a mist wrapping a flare.
I carry my precarious
heart, radiant and already
fading, out with me
along the tiled corridors
into the rest of the world,
which thinks it is opaque and hard.
I am being very careful.
O heart, now that I know your nature,
who can I tell?

A BOAT

Evening comes on and the hills thicken;
red and yellow bleaching out of the leaves.
The chill pines grow their shadows.

Below them the water stills itself,
a sunset shivering in it.
One more going down to join the others.

Now the lake expands
and closes in, both.

The blackness that keeps itself
under the surface in daytime
emerges from it like mist
or as mist.

Distance vanishes, the absence
of distance pushes against the eyes.

There is no seeing the lake,
only the outlines of the hills
which are almost identical,

familiar to me as sleep,
shores unfolding upon shores
in their contours of slowed breathing.

It is touch I go by,
the boat like a hand feeling
through shoals and among
dead trees, over the boulders
lifting unseen, layer
on layer of drowned time falling away.

This is how I learned to steer
through darkness by no stars.

To be lost is only a failure of memory.

INTERLUNAR

Darkness waits apart from any occasion for it;
like sorrow it is always available.
This is only one kind,

the kind in which there are stars
above the leaves, brilliant as steel nails
and countless and without regard.

We are walking together
on dead wet leaves in the intermoon
among the looming nocturnal rocks
which would be pinkish gray
in daylight, gnawed and softened
by moss and ferns, which would be green,
in the musty fresh yeast smell
of trees rotting, earth returning
itself to itself

and I take your hand, which is the shape a hand
would be if you existed truly.
I wish to show you the darkness
you are so afraid of.

Trust me. This darkness
is a place you can enter and be
as safe in as you are anywhere;
you can put one foot in front of the other
and believe the sides of your eyes.
Memorize it. You will know it
again in your own time.
When the appearances of things have left you,
you will still have this darkness.
Something of your own you can carry with you.

We have come to the edge:
the lake gives off its hush;
in the outer night there is a barred owl
calling, like a moth
against the ear, from the far shore
which is invisible.
The lake, vast and dimensionless,
doubles everything, the stars,
the boulders, itself, even the darkness
that you can walk so long in
it becomes light.

New Poems

1985–1986

AGING FEMALE POET SITS
ON THE BALCONY

The front lawn is littered with young men
who want me to pay attention to them
not to their bodies and their freshly-
washed cotton skins, not to their enticing
motifs of bulb and root, but
to their poems. In the back yard
on the other hand are the older men
who want me to pay attention to their
bodies. Ah men,
why do you want
all this attention?
I can write poems for myself, make
love to a doorknob if absolutely
necessary. What do you have to offer me
I can't find otherwise
except humiliation? Which I no longer
need. I gather
dust, for practice, my attention
wanders like a household pet
once leashed, now
out on the prowl, an animal
neither dog nor cat, unique
and hairy, snuffling
among the damp leaves at the foot
of the hedge, among the afterbloom
of irises which melt like blue and purple
ice back into air; hunting for something
lost, something to eat or love, among
the twists of earth,
among the glorious bearclaw sunsets, evidence
of the red life that is leaking
out of me into time, which become
each night more final.

PORCUPINE TREE

A porcupine tree is always
dead or half dead with chewed core
and mangy bark. Droppings drool down it.
In winter you can see it clear:
shreds of wood, porcupine piss
as yellow ice, toothwork, trails to and from
waddling in the snow. In summer you smell it.
This tree
is bigger than the other trees,
frowsy as my
room or my vocabulary.
It does not make
leaves much any more,
only porcupines and porcupines,
fat, slow and lazy,
each one a low note, the longest string
on a cello,
or like turning over in bed
under the eiderdown in spring,
early before the leaves are out;
sunlight too hot on you through the window,
your head sodden with marshy dreams
or like a lungfish burrowed
into mud. Oh pigsheart. Oh luxury.

I'll come around at night
and gnaw the salt off your hands,
eat toilet seats and axe handles.
That is my job in life: to sniff
your worn skin music,
to witness the border
between flesh and the inert,
lick up dried blood
soaked into the grain,
the taste of mortality in the wood.

AGING FEMALE POET READS
LITTLE MAGAZINES

Amazingly young beautiful woman poets
with a lot of hair falling down around
their faces like a bad ballet,
their eyes oblique over their cheekbones;
they write poems like blood in a dead person
that comes out black, or at least deep
purple, like smashed grapes.
Perhaps I was one of them once.
Too late to remember
the details, the veils.
If I were a man I would want to console them,
and would not succeed.

PORCUPINE MEDITATION

I used to have tricks, dodges, a whole sackful.
I could outfox anyone,
double back, cover my tracks,
walk backwards, the works.
I left it somewhere, that knack
of running, that good luck.

Now I have only
one trick left: head down, spikes out,
brain tucked in.
I can roll up:
thistle as animal, a flower of quills,
that's about it.

I lie in the grass and watch the sunlight pleating
the skin on the backs of my hands
as if I were a toad, squashed and drying.

I don't even wade through spring water
to cover my scent.
I can't be bothered.

I squat and stink, thinking:
peace and quiet are worth something.
Here I am, dogs,
nose me over,
go away sneezing, snouts full of barbs
hooking their way to your brain.
Now you've got some
of my pain. Much good may it do you.

AGING FEMALE POET ON LAUNDRY DAY

I prop up my face and go out, avoiding the sunlight,
keeping away from the curve where the burnt road
touches the sky.
Whatever exists at the earth's center will get me
sooner or later. Sooner. Than I think.
That core of light squeezed tight
and shut, dense as a star, as molten
mirrors. Dark red and heavy. Slab at the butcher's.
Already it's dragging me down, already
I become shorter, infinitesimally.
The bones of my legs thicken — that's first —
contract, like muscles.
After that comes the frailty, a dry wind blowing
inside my body,
scouring me from within, as if I were
a fossil, the soft parts eaten away.
Soon I will turn to calcium. It starts with the heart.

I do a lot of washing. I wash everything.
If I could only get this clean once, before I die.

To see God, they told me, you do not go
into the forest or city; not the meadow,
the seashore even unless it is cold.
You go to the desert.
You think of sand.

NIGHTSHADE ON THE WAY TO SCHOOL

Nightshade grows more densely than most weeds:
in the country of burdock and random stones,
rooted in undersides of damp logs,
leaf mold, worm castings.
Dark foliage, strong tendrils, the flowers purple
for mourning but with a center
so yellow I thought *buttercup* or *adder*,
the berries red, translucent,
like the eggs of an unknown moth,
feather-soft, nocturnal.
Belladonna was its name, *beautiful lady*.
Its other name was *deadly*.
If you ate it it would stop your heart,
you would sleep forever. I was told that.
Sometimes it was used for healing,
or in the eyes. I learned that later.

I had to go down the mud path to the ravine,
the wooden bridge across it rotting,
walk across it, from good
board to good board,
level with the tips of the trees.
Birds I don't remember.
On the other side the thicket of nightshade
where cats hunted, leaving their piss:
a smell of ammonia and rust, some dead thing.
All this in sunshine.

At that time I did well, my fingers
were eaten down to the blood.
They never healed.
The word *Nightshade* a shadow,
the color of a recurring dream
in which you cannot see color.
Porridge, worn underwear, wool
stockings, my fault. Not purple: some
other color. Sick
outside in a snowbank.

I dreamed of falling from the bridge,
one hand holding on, unable to call.
In other dreams, I could step into the air.
It was not flying. I never flew.

Now some years I cross the new bridge,
concrete, the path white gravel.
The old bridge is gone,
the nightshade has been cut down.
The nightshade spreads and thickens
where it always was,
at this season the red berries.
You would be tempted to eat them
if you did not know better.
Also the purple flowers.

MOTHERS

How much havoc this woman spills
out of herself into us
merely by being
unhappy with such finality:

The mothers rise up in us,
rustling, uttering cooing
sounds, their hands moving
into our hands, patting anything
smooth again. Her deprived eyes and deathcamp
shoulders. There there

we say, bringing
bright things in desperation:
a flower? We make
dolls of other people and offer
them to her. Have him, we say,
what about her? Eat their heads off
for all we care, but stop crying.

She half sits in the bed, shaking
her head under the cowl of hair.
Nothing will do, ever.

She discards us, crumples down
into the sheets, twisting around
that space we can never
hope to fill,
hugging her true mother,
the one who left her here
not among us:
hugging her darkness.

SHE

The snake hunts and sinews
his way along and is not his own
idea of viciousness. All he wants is
a fast grab, with fur and a rapid
pulse, so he can take that fluttering
and make it him, do a transfusion.
They say *whip* or *rope* about him, but this
does not give the idea; nor
phallus, which has no bones,
kills nothing and cannot see.
The snake sees red, like a hand held
above sunburn. Zeroes in,
which means, aims for the round egg
with nothing in it but blood.
If lucky, misses the blade
slicing light just behind him.
He's our idea of a bad time, we are his.
I say *he* out of habit. It could be *she*.

WEREWOLF MOVIES

Men who imagine themselves covered with fur and sprouting
fangs, why do they do that? Padding among wet
moonstruck treetrunks crouched on all fours, sniffing
the mulch of sodden leaves, or knuckling
their brambly way, arms dangling like outsized
pajamas, hair all over them, noses and lips
sucked back into their faces, nothing left of their kindly
smiles but yellow eyes and a muzzle. This gives them
pleasure, they think they'd be
more animal. Could then freely growl, and tackle
women carrying groceries, opening
their doors with keys. Freedom would be
bared ankles, the din of tearing: rubber, cloth,
whatever. Getting down to basics. Peel, they say
to strippers, meaning: take off the skin.
A guzzle of flesh
dogfood, ears in the bowl. But
no animal does that: couple and kill,
or kill first: rip up its egg, its future.
No animal eats its mate's throat, except
spiders and certain insects, when it's the protein
male who's gobbled. Why do they have this dream then?
Dress-ups for boys, some last escape
from having to be lawyers? Or a
rebellion against the mute
resistance of objects: reproach of the
pillowcase big with pillow, the tea-
cosy swollen with its warm
pot, not soft as it looks but hard
as it feels, round tummies of saved string in the top
drawer tethering them down. What joy, to smash the
tyranny of the doorknob, sink your teeth
into the inert defiant eiderdown with matching
spring-print queensized sheets and listen to her
scream. Surrender.

HOW TO TELL ONE COUNTRY FROM ANOTHER

Whether it is possible to become lost.

Whether one tree looks like another.
Whether there is water all around
the edges or not. Whether
there are edges or whether
there are just insects.

Whether the insects bite,
whether you would die
from the bites of the insects.
Whether you would die.

Whether you would die for your country.
Whether anyone in the country would die for your country.
Let's be honest here.
A layer of snow, a layer of granite, a layer of snow.
What you think lies under the snow.
What you think lies.

Whether you think white on white is a state of mind
or blue on blue or green on green.
Whether you think there is a state,
of mind.

How many clothes you have to take off
before you can make love.
This I think is important:
the undoing of buttons, the gradual shedding
of one color after another. It leads
to the belief that what you see is not
what you get.

Whether there are preliminaries,
hallways, vestibules,
basements, furnaces,
chesterfields, silences
between sentences, between pieces
of furniture, parasites in your eyes,
drinkable water.

Whether there has ever been
an invading army.
Whether, if there were an invading army,
you would collaborate.
Poor boy, you'd say, he looks cold
standing out there, and he's only twenty.
From his point of view this must be hell.

A fur coat is what he needs,
a cup of tea, a cup of coffee,
a warm body.
Whether on the contrary
you'd slit his throat in his sleep
or in yours. I ask you.

So, you are a nice person.
You would behave well.
What you mean by behaving well.
When the outline of a man
whose face you cannot see
appears at your bedroom window,
whether you would shoot.
If you had a gun, that is.
Whether you would have a gun.
It goes on.

MACHINE. GUN. NEST.

The blood goes through your neck veins with a noise they call singing.
Time shatters like bad glass; you are this pinpoint of it.

Your feet rotting inside your boots, the skin of your chest
festering under the zippers, the waterproof armor,

you sit here, on the hill, a vantage point, at this X or scuffling
in the earth, which they call a nest. Who chose that word?

Whatever you are you are not an egg, or a bird either.
Vipers perhaps is what was meant. Who cares now?

That is the main question: who cares. Not these pieces of paper
from somewhere known as *home* you fold, unread, in your pocket.

Each landscape is a state of mind, he once told me:
mountains for awe and remoteness, meadows for calm and the steam

of the lulled senses. But some views are slippery.
This place is both beautiful as the sun and full of menace:

dark green, with now and then a red splotch, like a punctured
vein, white like a flare; stench of the half-eaten.
Look at it carefully, see what it hides, or it will burst in your head.

If you lose your nerve you may die, if you don't lose it
you may die anyway, the joke goes. What is your nerve?

It is turning the world flat, the moon to a disc you could aim at,
popping the birds off the fence wire. Delight in accuracy,

no attention paid to results, dead singing, the smear of feathers.
You know you were more than that, but best to forget it.

There's no slack time for memory here; when you can, you plunge
into some inert woman as into a warm bath; for a moment
comforting, and of no consequence, like sucking your thumb.

No woman can imagine this. What you do to them
is therefore incidental, and also your just reward,

though sometimes, in a gap in the action, there's a space
for the concepts of *sister, mother*. Like folded laundry. They come
    and go.

But stick your hand up a woman, alive or freshly-
dead, it is much like a gutted chicken:
giblets, a body cavity. Killing can be

merely a kind of impatience, at the refusal
of this to mean anything to you. He told me that.

You wanted to go in sharp and clean with a sword,
do what they once called battle. Now you just want your life.

There's not much limit to what you would do to get it.
Justice and mercy are words that happen in cool rooms, elsewhere.

Are you your brother's keeper? Yes or no, depending
what clothes he has on, what hair. There is more than one brother.

What you need to contend with now is the hard Easter-
eggshell blue of the sky, that shows you too clearly

the mass of deep green trees leaning slowly towards you
as if on the verge of speech, or annunciation.

More likely some break in the fabric of sight, or a sad mistake
you will hear about in the moment you make it. Some glint of
    reflected light.

That whir in the space where your left hand was is not singing.
Death is the bird that hatches, is fed, comes flying.

THE REST

The rest of us watch from beyond the fence
as the woman moves with her jagged stride
into her pain as if into a slow race.
We see her body in motion
but hear no sounds, or we hear
sounds but no language; or we know
it is not a language we know
yet. We can see her clearly
but for her it is running in black smoke.
The clusters of cells in her swelling
like porridge boiling, and bursting,
like grapes, we think. Or we think of
explosions in mud; but we know nothing.
All around us the trees
and the grasses light up with forgiveness,
so green and at this time
of the year healthy.
We would like to call something
out to her. Some form of cheering.
There is pain but no arrival at anything.

ANOTHER ELEGY

Strawberries, pears, fingers, the eyes
of snails: the other shapes water
takes. Even leaves are liquid
arrested. To die
is to dry, lose juice,
the sweet pulp sucked out. To enter
the time of rind and stone.

Your clothes hang shriveling
in the closet, your other body once
filled with your breath.
When I say *body*, what
is that a word for?
Why should the word *you*
remain attached to that suffering?
Wave upon wave, as we say.

I think of your hair burning
first, a scant minute
of halo; later, an afterglow
of bone, red slash of sunset.
The body a cinder or luminescent
saint, or Turner seascape.

Fine words, but why do I want
to tart up death?
Which needs no decoration,
which is only a boat,
plain and wooden
and ordinary, without eyes
painted on it,
sightless and hidden
in fog and going somewhere
else. Away from the shore.

My dear, my voyager, my scant handful
of ashes: I'd scatter you
if I could, this way, on the river.
A wave is neither form
nor energy. Both. Neither.

GALIANO COAST: FOUR ENTRANCES

i

The arbutus trees, with their bark like burned skin
that has healed, enclosing someone's real arms
in the moment of reaching, but not towards you:

you know they are paying no attention
to you and your failed love and equivocation.

Why do you wish to be forgiven by them?
Yet you are, and you breathe in,
and the new moon sheds grace without intention.

ii

You lie on your stomach
looking down through a crack between rocks:

the seaweed with its bladders and hairs,
the genital bodies hinted
by the pink flanges of limpets,
five starfish, each thickened purple arm
a drowning tongue,
the sea's membrane, with its wet shine
and pulse, and no promise.

There is no future,
really there is none
and no salvation

To know this is salvation

iii

Where the rock stops upland, thistles burning
at the tips, leaving their white ash

A result of the sun, this pentecost
and conflagration.

Light flares up off the tidepool
where the barnacles grasp at the water
each with its one skeletal hand
which is also a frond

which is also a tongue
which is also a flame
you are praised by

iv

Sandrock the color of erosion,
pushed by the wind
into gills and clefts
and heavy folds like snow melting
or the crease of a doubled arm

There ought to be caves here

The sunlight
slides over the body like pollen

A door is about to open
onto paradise. Onto a beach like this one,

exactly like it, down to each thistle,
down to the red halfcrab eaten on the sand,
down to the rubber glove
gone white and blinded,
wedged in and stranded by the tide

down to the loss because you
can never truly be here.

Can this be paradise, with so much loss
in it?

      Paradise
is defined by loss.
                      Is loss.
Is.

SQUAW LILIES: SOME NOTES

Went up the steep stone hill, thinking,
My trick hip could fail me. Went up anyway
to see the flower with three names:
chocolate lilies, for the color,
stink lilies for the smell, red meat going off,
squaw lilies. Thought what I would be like, falling.
Brain spilled on the rocks.
Said to her: never seen these before. Why squaw?
Oh, she said, something to do
with the smell.
When she said that I felt as if painted
naked on an off-blue sofa
by a bad expressionist, ochre
and dirty greens, lips thickened with yellow
pigment, a red-infected
crevice dividing the splayed legs.
Thought: this is what it is, to be part
of the landscape. Subject to
depiction. Thought:
release the lilies. They have nothing
to do with these names for them.
Not even lilies.
Went down the steep stone hill. Did not fall.

THREE PRAISES

*

The dipper, small dust-colored bird with robin
feet, walks on the stream bed
enclosed in its nimbus of silver
air, miraculous bubble, a non-miracle.
Who could have thought it? We think it now,
and liverwort on a dead log, earthstar,
hand, finger by finger.

*

For you, at last, I'd like to make
something uncomplicated; some neither god
nor goddess, not between, beyond
them; pinch it from dough,
bake it in the oven, a stone in its belly.
Stones lined up on the windowsill,
picked off some beach or other for being holy.

*

The hookworm, in the eye of
the universe, which is the unsteady gaze
of eternity maybe, is beloved. How could it not be,
living so blessed, in its ordained red meadows
of blood where it waves like a seaweed?
Praise be, it sings with its dracula mouth.
Praise be.

NOT THE MOON

What idiocy could transform the moon, that old sea-overgrown
skull seen from above, to a goddess of mercy?

You fish for the silver light, there on the quiet lake, so clear
to see; you plunge your hands into the water and come up empty.

Don't ask questions of stones. They will rightly ignore you,
they have shoulders but no mouths, their conversation is elsewhere.

Expect nothing else from the perfect white birdbones, picked clean
in the sedge in the cup of muskeg: you are none of their business.

Fresh milk in a glass on a plastic tray, a choice of breakfast
foods; we sit at the table, discussing the theories of tragedy.

The plump pink-faced men in the metal chairs at the edge of the
   golf course
adding things up, sunning themselves, adding things up.

The corpse, washed and dressed, beloved meat pumped full of
   chemicals
and burned, if turned back into money could feed two hundred.

Voluptuousness of the newspaper; scratching your back on the
   bad news;
furious anger in spring sunshine, a plate of fruit on the table.

Ask of the apple, crisp heart, ask the pear or suave banana
which necks got sucked, whose flesh got stewed, so we could love
   them.

The slug, a muscular jelly, slippery and luminous, dirty
eggwhite unrolling its ribbon of mucous — this too is delicious.

The oily slick, rainbow-colored, spread on the sewage
flats in the back field is beautiful also

as is the man's hand cut off at the wrist and nailed to a treetrunk,
mute and imploring, as if asking for alms, or held up in warning.

Who knows what it tells you? It does not say, beg, *Have mercy*,
it is too late for that. Perhaps only, *I too was here once, where you are.*

The star-like flower by the path, by the ferns, in the rain-
forest, whose name I did not know, and the war in the jungle —

the war in the jungle, blood on the crushed ferns, whose name I
  do not
know, and the star-like flower grow out of the same earth

whose name I do not know. Whose name for itself I do not know.
Or much else, except that the moon is no goddess of mercy

but shines on us each damp warm night of her full rising
as if she were, and that is why we keep asking

the wrong questions, he said, of the wrong things. The questions
  of things.
                                                    Ask the spider
what is the name of God, she will tell you: God is a spider.

Let the other moons pray to the moon. O Goddess of Mercy,
you who are not the moon, or anything we can see clearly,

we need to know each other's names and what we are asking.
Do not be any thing. Be the light we see by.

BODILY HARM

'A magnificent novel of intrigue and betrayal'
Options

THE HANDMAID'S TALE

A major film starring Faye Dunaway,
Robert Duvall & Natasha Richardson
Shortlisted for the Booker Prize
Winner of the Arthur C. Clarke Award for Science
Fiction Over a million copies sold worldwide

'Superlative'
Angela Carter

CAT'S EYE

'Not since Graham Greene or William Golding
has a novelist captured so forcefully the
relationship between school bully and victim . . .
Atwood's power games are played, exquisitely,
by little girls'
Listener

DANCING GIRLS

'If anyone has better insight into women and their central problem – men – than Margaret Atwood, and can voice them with as much wit, impact and grace, then they haven't started writing yet'
Daily Mail

BLUEBEARD'S EGG

'Sophisticated, reticent, ornate, stark, supple, stiff, savage or forgiving; they are exactly what she wants them to be. They are stories from the prime of life'
Times Literary Supplement

WILDERNESS TIPS

A third collection of short stories, is forthcoming in 1992.

Poetry by Margaret Atwood

'A wordchild with the gift of tongues, puns, echoes and symbols' – *The Times*

POEMS 1965–1975
With a New Introduction by the Author

The evolution of Margaret Atwood's poetry illuminates one of our major literary talents. Here, as in her novels, is intensity combined with sardonic detachment, and in these early poems her genius for a level stare at the ordinary is already apparent – as is her startling ability to contrast the everyday with the terrifying.